All The Reasons Why You Should Be Paying 6% Commission to Sell Your Home!

Donald Gorbach

Copyright © 2018 by Donald Gorbach

All rights reserved.

ISBN-10 1725822784
ISBN-13 978-1725822788

A Top Real Estate Broker was just on a listing for a $7 million home. When Seller said, "Let's talk about your commission. You certainly aren't worth $420,000."

The veteran and respected Broker thought to himself, "He's right... of course I'm not, but how do I justify this preposterous amount"?

REALITYCOVERBOOKS.COM

INTRODUCTION

The reason why this book has blank pages is because truthfully, there are no reasons to justify to a homeowner that he/she should be paying a 6% commission to sell their house or condo based on the following:

FACT: More than $65 Billion Dollars were paid in real estate commissions nationwide!

FACT: The 6% Commission hasn't changed in over 50 Years!

FACT: In 1970, The Median Home Price was $23K with a Commission of $1,380

FACT: In 2017, The Median Home Price was $235K with a Commission of $14,100

FACT: The Cost of Real Estate Marketing has gone down SUBSTANTIALLY over the Years, thanks to the Internet and the elimination of expensive print advertising.

FACT: 95% of All Homebuyers search online for their own home today.

FACT: AGENTS ARE DOING LESS WORK, SPENDING LESS ON MARKETING AND ADVERTISING, BUT GETTING PAID MORE THAN EVER BEFORE!

TAKE-AWAY:
THE 6% REAL ESTATE MODEL JUST DOESN'T MAKE SENSE ANYMORE!

www.ingramcontent.com/pod-product-compliance
Lightning Source LLC
Chambersburg PA
CBHW071538220526
45469CB00003B/830